EmpowerMe

Life Skills 101: Beyond the Classroom

by Joe Villmow

Copyright © 2017 by Joseph Villmow

All rights reserved. Printed in the United States. No part of this book may be reproduced or transmitted in any form or by any means without written permission from the author or publisher.

Designed by Ssali Media Group.

In honor of my late grandmother, Cecelia Haro, who inspired, mentored and believed in me. I learned to be successful isn't about a monetary benefit, it is about the rewards you reap you inspire others to become a better version of themselves.

Table of Contents

Foreword

Introduction

Chapter 1	Communicating with People	23
Chapter 2	The World is Changing	29
Chapter 3	A New Way	35
Chapter 4	The Meaning of Success...and Failure	45
Chapter 5	Plan to Be Empowered	61
Chapter 6	Encouragement versus Motivation	69
Chapter 7	Personal Mission Statement	77
Chapter 8	Academic Success or Failure: ...It's Up to You	85
Chapter 9	Networking	95
Chapter 10	Keeping the Conversation Going	103
Chapter 11	Mentoring Basics	111
Chapter 12	Questions for Your Mentor	117
Chapter 13	Planning on Success	123
Chapter 14	Andres	131
Chapter 15	The Compound Effect	139
Chapter 16	Conclusion	149

Foreword

Since 1997, Joe Villmow has been my mentee. He joined the UMOS Board of Directors, representing youth, and with his drive for connecting others, became one of the youngest board members. Our mission at UMOS is to provide programs and services to under-served populations. We are able to forge ahead in our work each day based on the bridges we build for others. Understanding the value of bridges and networking as Joe's mentor, I have purposefully introduced him to people and groups around the country. He has joined me at a number of national conferences including the following, National Council of La Raza (NCLR), now UnidosUS; League of United Latin American Citizens (LULAC), and MAFO (a national partnership of farmworker organizations). At these conferences, he has gained access to treasured networking opportunities during banquets, lunches, and receptions.

I enjoy observing Joe's philanthropic side as he volunteers for community serving events including Mexican Fiesta – raising funds and extending his leadership to Hispanic students in the area – along with the UMOS Mexican Independence Day Parade and Festival. Because of the responsibility he's shown through UMOS Board of Directors service and Mexican Fiesta, I have begun to transition my overall responsibility of management of several hundred volunteers to his capable hands. Once I step aside from this role completely, I am confident that Joe will continue its mission to serve the community through scholarship fundraising and run the event smooth. A key area of Joe's involvement and active participation is the UMOS Board of Directors, where I value his input with agency affairs. Joe's success has been an inspiration. With the success of our mentor/mentee relationship, others have stepped forward asking if they could be a future mentee.

The skills that Joe has acquired from our relationship shaped him to develop his own professional relationships with his EmpowerME Foundation. He sees the value of guiding young people to recognize the importance of pursuing their educational goals. Joe also impresses upon young people the importance of volunteering in their respective communities. He appreciates the idea that someone has helped him, and he can then help others in the same or similar manner in their life.

This book will tell people the behind the scenes story of the struggles Joe has encountered. In spite of his challenges, he was able to overcome and obtain his goals, educationally, professionally and personally. What may seem to be an easy task for most students, was monumental for Joe, but through his perseverance he found success. Clearly, he is able to explain to his readers that if he was able to succeed, so can they. His other clear messages are to never give up, and do not be afraid to ask for help.

Interestingly enough, when I first met Joe, he had come into my office, talked to my Executive Assistant and asked if he could meet with me. He did not have an appointment, my Assistant asked him the purpose of his presence at our organization. She informed him he would have to schedule a future appointment. He did. On the day of the appointment, I asked Joe, the purpose of the meeting and who had referred him. He told me, "My Grandma sent me."

I have known Joe's grandparents for many years. Jesse Haro, Joe's Grandfather, was the Commander of the David Valdez Post, a Latino Veteran's Organization. Cecelia Haro, Joe's Grandma, was in charge of the women's auxiliary for the post. I supported and sponsored many of their events over the years. Joe's Grandma had told him that I was someone who might be able to help him achieve his personal mission. "It's not what you know, it's who you know," his Grandma said. So when I asked the young man I've come to know as Joey, "How can I help you?" Joey replied, "My Grandma wants me to ask you to be my mentor." The rest is history.

Joe is great at networking, and can often be seen working the room and sharing his knowledge while meeting new people. He has great plans for his future in the area of business development and because of the skills and knowledge he has picked up along the way, I am confident he will succeed.

My advice to anyone reading this book for the next 5 to 10 years is similar to what I told Joe many years ago.

1. Continue to do what you do so well, which is to be persistent.

2. Do not take on too many projects all at once.

3. Focus on those areas that are the most important to you.

4. Move things forward methodically.

5. Work hard to achieve them through good planning.

Lupe Martinez
President and Chief Executive Officer, UMOS

"Nothing in the world can take the place of persistence.

Talent will not; nothing is more common than unsuccessful men with talent. Genius will not; unrewarded genius is almost a proverb.

Education will not; the world is full of educated derelicts.

Persistence and **determination** alone are omnipotent.

The slogan *Press On!* has solved and always will solve the problems of the human race."

Calvin Coolidge
30th United States President
—

Introduction
Turn Can't Into Can

What do you do when someone tells you, you can't? You're not smart enough? What's your plan when the only person who empowers you…is you?

It was in the 7th grade that I identified and figured out my life goal. I wanted to attend Marquette University in Milwaukee, Wisconsin. I was rejected for admission the first time I applied. I heard an echo through my head. Can't attend. *Can't.*

Spoiler alert on how my educational journey ended. I am a proud Marquette University graduate and entrepreneur. *Can. And Did.* The journey might have been easy…had I not been dyslexic.

I decided to tackle my challenges head on and through grit, hard work and determination, achieved my goal. If I did it, no doubt you can too. This book is here to empower YOU. I founded EmpowerMe Foundation out of a personal mission to help young people fulfill their goals and dreams in spite of the many obstacles that may stand in their way.

As a middle and high school student and even in college, however, I experienced lots of setbacks and frustrations. With the help of family and friends, I learned to manage my learning disability.

I've become a successful business owner and independent distributor of grocery products. I've owned and operated security-related company since 1998, and I have experience in both property and facility management. It might seem like a lot of work, and it is. It's not easy.

When I look at issues young people face today, it reminds me of the struggles I faced growing up. Eventually, I learned success came through understanding and mastering soft skills, which is one reason why I'm writing this book.

Inside, you will be asked to journal about wins, loses, challenges, memories and struggles that have helped make you the person you are today. These issues will also help make you become the person you were meant to be. It all starts here.

EmpowerME Journal Topic

Describe any challenges or struggles you hope to overcome by reading this book.

_____

_____

_____

_____

_____

_____

_____

"The art of
communication
is the language of
leadership."

James Humes
Author

—

1

Communicating with People

I think the problem with young people today may be a combination of things – a lack of soft skills and a lack of life skills. I believe this is caused by a lot of young people being given things they did not earn the hard way. Teachers should empower students to figure problems out on their own. The same goes for parents. If the student can't get their way at home, they may act out.

Students can hide behind technology through apps, email, and texting. They forget that important communication happens when you speak to someone face-to-face. Many young people go on their computers and phones to write how they feel. In the long run, this really doesn't help. Sure, you get it off your chest, but bullies may pick on you because of what you said using technology, and it's hard to defend yourself against a social media page.

When it comes to using technology to communicate, the way young people use technology is spilling over into their school work. Abbreviations, broken words and slang are now used, and accepted, in school work.

When professional communication is needed, many students use the same unprofessional habit of communication they use with family and friends. They may believe this type of communication is okay. I'm here to tell you—it's wrong.

It's important to communicate with others clearly and effectively. Use what you're learning in your English and Language Arts classes to help balance what you're typing into your social media.

When you get a chance to meet and network with executives in college and beyond, you'll be a step ahead of everyone else. Just by the words that accompany your handshake. Keep in mind that your social media posts, even the rants, could be viewed by college admissions and future employers.

EmpowerME Journal Topic

Describe three things you will do in an effort to communicate better with others.

_____

_____

_____

_____

_____

_____

_____

"If the facts
don't fit the theory,
change the facts."

Albert Einstein
Theoretical Physicist

—

2

The World is Changing

Today, a student who emails and texts professionals in the workplace the same casual way they email and text family and friends, is being unprofessional. This is evident when they apply for jobs. "IMO" has no place in an employment or college application.

Being a business owner and having talked to other business owners, I hear the same comments over and over—young people lack soft skills. They lack the ability to communicate. They lack problem solving skills. They lack the basics of networking. Schools and colleges talk about it, yet don't teach how to get a job and how to network. Colleges don't talk about life skills and tools needed to survive in the work world. Schools don't teach students how to brand themselves and be accountable. *Life Skills 101: Beyond The Classroom* will help give students the information they need to be professional in today's workplaces and into the future. Let's take the time now to turn *can't* learn soft skills into can.

I completed this book to share with young people my experiences that helped me be successful. My experiences in middle school, high school and college where so-so at best, but I wish I'd learned some things I learned later in life, sooner. It was a shock to realize once I got deeper into college and the work world, how much I didn't know. I lacked the ability to hold a conversation with anyone, let alone a CEO.

I found, after speaking to people ranging from other Marquette students to the Marquette University Board of Directors, the skill of communication has to be learned. This book can be used as a "bible" of sorts to help guide you on how to act and speak when you meet new people.

It may be helpful to think about this book in terms of changing the way you communicate with adults. No one wants to feel silly when holding a conversation. Your mind might drift to all of the things you might not know. Or how to break the ice with people you just met. In *Life Skills 101: Beyond The Classroom*, you will learn how to build the foundation needed to hold a conversation, move you out of your comfort zone, and gain new skills. This a book about the basics.

EmpowerME Journal Topic

Describe what fears you may have when dealing with change.

_____

_____

_____

_____

_____

_____

_____

"Trust is the glue of life.
It's the most essential ingredient
in effective communication.
It's the foundational principle
that holds all relationships."

Stephen Covey
American Educator

—

A New Way

Reading this book will give students the knowledge needed to ask the right questions in life. My main focus in high school was to have a personal mission statement, knowing where I want to go in life, and achieving this goal. Having a statement, asking the right questions, and learning from others allows you to use this knowledge. Don't forget, when you meet others, you may get to know their friends and build relationships.

Does reading this book guarantee you'll be successful in these new relationships? No. Yet, if you go back through the book and practice the steps given and use them repeatedly, they'll become second nature. The one step you take can be as simple as making a follow-up phone call or sending a thank-you note. It's the little things that make you stand out from everyone else.

We always hear teachers tell us, "It's all about the grades!"
I believe it's all about how you hold yourself together practicing the following steps:

1. A proper handshake
2. Being a leader.
3. Dressing appropriately.
4. Following up on an email.
5. Learning to communicate.
6. Listening.
7. Speaking well.

You Can Do It

My story, my life, my memory are ones of struggle. I have dyslexia, meaning I have trouble interpreting written words, letters and symbols. It is not a reflection of my intelligence, otherwise this book would have not be written. The keyword here is struggle.

There are several other things you have to know about me. I never thought I would go to college. I became a bully because teachers would ask me to read aloud in classes, and when I stumbled and could not, kids laughed and picked on me. This went on for a while until a teacher I met changed my life.

As students, we forget that the people who care about us are the people who are the hardest on us. The teacher spoke to me about my outbursts and bullying at school. I told the teacher, "Go &$&%^$ yourself!"

Needless to say, the teacher put me in my place, and the thing that changed my life is his personal story. This teacher was dyslexic like me, and overcame. He turned his *can't* into *can*. He was empowered.

He graduated from Marquette. He lost both of his parents while in college. He asked me the question, "If I can do it, why can't you?" He told me the decision to change, achieve and be successful was up to me and added an important piece to my life. He told me, "I am here to support you." Today, I say to you as you read this book: It is up to you to change your circumstances and be successful.

Support allowed me to be able to write my personal mission statement in the seventh grade, to go to Marquette, take over my Dad's business, and give back to the community. In all honesty, I didn't think I would accomplish any of these things, because in seventh grade, I didn't have a clue as to how to begin this journey. In seventh grade you do what you are supposed to do; you do what your parents tell you to do.

Down the road of life, people told me I was not smart enough to go to Marquette. In fact, teachers told me I could not go to college. Even my parents, whom I believe love me with all their heart, told me I could not go to Marquette because I was not smart enough. My parents suggested I go to another school, or go to a two-year college. And yet, when you are determined, you can make anything happen.

Going to Marquette was not easy. I was rejected the first time I applied to attend college. I cried to my Grandmother (I was a Grandma's boy) and she told me, "What did I tell you? It's about knowing the right person who can give you the edge to make it and get you in." Taking her advice, I reached out to people who helped me in the past, and to this day, I owe them everything. These are the people who supported me, and helped create the opportunity to attend Marquette and be successful in achieving my educational goal.

I am thankful for my education. I took advantage of the opportunity. I did not give up, and realized there is always a way to get what you want. You have to think about what you want, and be determined to be successful.

For me, success was turning a "no" into a "yes." After high school, I had to go to summer school. Once in college, my journey got even tougher. Nine people who were close to me, passed away over the course of three years. I wanted to give up, and wished I was not alive. I wished it was all over, but I remembered that others fought for my opportunity to attend college, and I would not let them down. I realized that if I let them down, it may change how the people who helped me ultimately helped others. My actions might stop them from helping others because of their negative experience with me. This thought drove me to success. In the end, when someone opens a door for you, appreciate it.

Keep Going

People supported me and believed in me. Even when I wanted to give up, I could not. My reason for not giving up is realizing God has a plan for everyone's life. I know there are obstacles in everyone's life. How you overcome the obstacles of can't will decide who you can become in life.

Looking back, I am grateful God put these obstacles in my way. Obstacles made me into a better person. That's why I am sharing this book. I want this book to show you that you have a purpose in life. I realize you may have more obstacles in your life than I will, and may be living a tougher life each day. However, I am living proof that you can make it.

If you come from a single-parent household or poverty, or a great home, there are people who will support and help you. The key ingredient in all of this is you have to want it. You have to ask the right questions in life to get the right answers. That's how you'll be empowered to move beyond the classroom into the real world.

An Overview

As I stated before, this book will do several things for you. First, it will help you develop a mission statement. It will help you figure out what you want out of life. You will learn how to identify your strengths and weaknesses. Then, you will learn how to develop lifelong positive habits. You will learn how to network. Also, you will learn the steps to finding a personal mentor.

I am convinced that if you learn these key components, you can change the trajectory of your life, make an impact in your community, and achieve your mission in life. I did.

EmpowerME Journal Topic

Describe why practice will make you more comfortable speaking to others.

_____

_____

_____

_____

_____

_____

_____

_____

"

"Almost everything comes from nothing."

Henry F. Amiel
Swiss Philosopher
—

4

The Meaning of Success...and Failure

Some people don't understand the meaning of success. In high school, I believed that success was reflected in the following ways:

- The amount of money you are saving
- The amount of your salary
- The kind of car you drive
- The size of your house.

I believe the absolute best way you can measure success is to look at the way you understand success. Find your why.

'Why' is the question, 'why' is the goal, and the knowledge that comes from answering the question *why*, is also the outcome. Essentially, it may be enough to know what you want to accomplish in life. You figure out your goal, set it and move forward. However, it is essential you know 'why' you want to accomplish your goal.

The why is simply becoming what are you trying to accomplish in life so others can see it and use your path as a model. The why is doing what you love doing in life so you and others can be successful. In my journey, I figured out that my why is wanting to see empowered youth with the knowledge and experiences others sowed into me.

I recognize my success happened because I had great people who shared their lives with me. Struggling during my journey and working to overcome obstacles distracted me from connecting the goal to the why. I didn't understand why I wanted achieve the goal. My only goal was to make money and have a large home. I realized that to be successful, money and a large home are only part of the equation. Ultimately, the why manifested itself in the creation of the EmpowerMe Foundation.

The EmpowerMe Foundation's goal is to change the life of youth. Changing lives for the better is priceless. For me, changing lives is more important to me than earning money. Having spoken to a number of successful multi-millionaires, each of them have shared their belief that money is not the most important aspect of life.

I listened and I now understand their point of view. When a person pursues money for the sake of having money, they tend to want more and more money.

What happens when you make your first million dollars at age 23? What do you want? What do you pursue? In many cases, you want to pursue more money. In this same arena, you want more power. There is a false sense or belief that money and power equal happiness. I am here to tell you that money and power do not equal happiness. Increased money brings increased issues.

To be fair, you can make money, achieve power do great things in life. There are people in the world who are wealthy and happy. Yet, I believe this may be the exception, not the rule.

A New Approach

The goal of this book is to assist you in discovering what you want in life, discovering what you want to achieve, and knowing why you want to achieve the goal. This approach comes from my experiences as far back as seventh grade where I created a personal mission statement.

The reason why I go all the way back to the seventh grade is to remember the teachers and parents who pushed me to succeed. I dare say, if you look in your past, a person who you believe can be described as hard, mean or tough, probably impacted your life in a positive way.

The words from a hard, mean and tough teacher made me believe the teacher was mean or a bully. In reality, the teacher wanted me be to be successful. At that time, he probably wanted my success more than I did. He pushed me to study as I kept saying, "You don't understand what I'm thinking. It doesn't matter how much I study, I still keep failing." He responded by sharing personal information that changed my life.

My teacher shared with me how he overcame his dyslexia. He also told me how he overcame it in the midst of losing both of his parents while attending college. After he told me, I was thinking exactly what he said…"If one person can do it, anybody can do it."

Then and Now

I believe when I was in school, I was hard on myself, but teachers and parents were a lot harder on all of us students. Today, if you're hard on a student, it ends up in the media. In all honesty, to be successful, I believe you need people surrounding you that will empower you by pushing you to higher standards. From that beginning, it will be up to you to learn yourself and what it takes to motivate yourself internally. What you say to yourself each day is more important than any other conversation you will have. A few years ago, after becoming successful in business, I asked myself, "How can I share what I've learned with students, so they don't have to learn at the school of hard knocks, like I did?"

In order to empower students, I began to think about these questions:

How do I help make students successful?

How do I help students grow beyond their current place in life?

What new approach can be used to help make students successful?

The Struggle

While the following words may sound harsh, the intent is not meant to be harsh – I believe students today need to do be encouraged to figure out life. Instead of being given answers, there needs to be a combination of teaching and practical experience. Education gives answers to certain knowledge. Additionally, students need to get their hands dirty and their feet wet. I believe wholeheartedly that with perseverance comes strength.

It's okay to struggle a bit to find your solutions in life. When incorrect choices are made, it is up to you and your valued circle to help you troubleshoot what is wrong and help find the solution that keeps you close to your core motivation.

Learning to ride a bicycle is a perfect example of the process. First, someone demonstrates a smooth ride. Next, they explain how to pedal and keep your balance. Then, you're guided to practice staying upright and moving forward. Steer straight ahead. Lastly, someone watched over your shoulder as you solidified your skills. You most likely continued to practice all summer until you became a master on two wheels.

You'll find throughout school, college and life, to get really good at anything means you'll have to see it in action, work with others to show you how to excel, and then practice like crazy. That's when you'll find success. Think of networking, finding a mentor and learning your craft to be like learning to ride a bike. *Life Skills 101: Beyond The Classroom* is your quick guide to learning how to ride and when you're out in the real world. You'll get to take the training wheels off and practice.

Remember the words of Mahatma Gandhi:

> **Your beliefs become your thoughts,**
> **Your thoughts become your words,**
> **Your words become your actions,**
> **Your actions become your habits,**
> **Your habits become your values,**
> **Your values become your destiny.**

Each day, you have to create habits that enable you to succeed. You have to develop soft skills in the area of public speaking and networking. These are the skills that give you the upper hand in life. Again, this book is a place to begin building the foundation for success. Reading this book builds a foundation upon which you practice day in and day out. With practice, you will be effective. Effectiveness, over time will in the end, yield a successful life.

"

"In taking this new approach, we must allow students to figure it out for themselves, and we must help them to develop a series of minor wins."

Joe Villmow
Author

—

Get Empowered to Win

When I was younger, it was difficult for me to see whether or not I was winning. I believed I was a monumental failure. Today, all of my failures amount to experience. For me, that's important.
I learned, grew from the experience, and not only did I succeed,
I believe I a making an impact on the world because I am a leader.

My hope is that in the coming months, you begin to share this book with other people. With the EmpowerMe Journal, I hope you'll shape your experience into your story.

It is important to understand that successful people didn't get that way because they're smart. They became successful because they failed, and refused to up. They persevered. But if you can take your experiences and be confident in your story, you'll have a chance to meet others. You can learn from them how **not** to give up when it seems dark and hopeless, when you don't understand the assignment, or feel awkward walking into a room and starting a conversation with strangers. I've seen a number of students, including myself, give up after a failure. Push yourself a bit harder.

It's about how you figure out and solve the problem, get back up and tackle life. It's the concept of remaining motivated when life says 'no' to you.

A Note on Losing

In a world where students become successful, they win. We've learned in life if there is a winner, there has to be a loser – or does anybody really lose? I don't think anyone loses. Working through life's struggles, and winning in the end means that students win, parents win, teachers win, and society wins. A perfect example is my decision to attend college. My grades were average and definitely not up to the level of Marquette University, and my ACT score was low. My parents didn't want to see me fail and I believe they were being protective when they encouraged me to attend a community college, or any other college or university that would take me. And yet, I figured it out.

The Moment

So many people said no to me, I wanted to prove them wrong. It was hard, and looking back, it was the most difficult time in my life.

One day it struck me like lightning. I realized I was the only person stopping me from doing anything. I was my own worst enemy. You may well be your own worst enemy. So, I looked in the mirror and asked myself the question – "How are you going to go to Marquette University?"

The question forced me to find a solution.

EmpowerME Journal Topic

Describe your idea of success…and failure.

"Knowledge is of no value… unless you put it to practice."

Anton Chekov
Russian Playwright
—

5

Plan to Be Empowered

The point of *Life Skills 101: Beyond The Classroom* is to give you information that helps you become successful in life and fulfill your dreams. First, there are a couple of things you need to know and remember.

Encouragement versus Motivation

Encouragement is foundational to motivation. Essentially, it is not enough to be encouraged. You have to turn encouragement into motivation.

Personal Mission Statement

The most awesome experience I've had was creating a personal mission statement. I'll show you the basics of a personal mission statement and how to use it for motivation.

Academic Success or Failure: It's Up to You

Three simple activities can spell academic success. Not completing three simple activities could spell academic failure. Which decision will you make? It's up to you.

Networking

Why is it so important to network? How do you network? Believe me, if I can learn to network…you can learn to network. I'll leave you with what I believe to be the best seven benefits to networking.

Keeping the Conversation Going

So, you learned how to network. You met someone you believe could change the trajectory of your life by becoming a mentor. You would talk to them…if you knew what to say. I will show you how I kept the conversation going.

What is a Mentor?

The most crucial relationship you may have, second only to your parents and teachers, is a mentoring relationship. Meeting people, speaking and holding conversations with people, and developing a mentoring relationship can start with an introduction.

I Have A Mentor: Now What?

This chapter of the book will help you discover what steps are needed to help shape the mentoring relationship.

Questions for Your Mentor

This chapter reveals how to develop the proper set of questions to ask your mentor.

Planning on Success

Taking time to review goals is important. A personal mission statement on paper gives you a road map in life. You can always change it later. One of my favorite quotes is by Benjamin Franklin, who said it well, "By failing to prepare, you are preparing to fail." Plan to succeed. Read the chapters and enjoy "The Pizza Plan."

EmpowerME Journal Topic

Describe which chapter or topic in this book you believe will be most important for your success in life.

_____

_____

_____

_____

_____

_____

_____

_____

"Motivation is what gets
you started.

Habit is what keeps
you going."

Jim Ryun
American Olympic Athlete
—

6

Encouragement versus Motivation

Encouragement comes from others, those who believe in you and support your goals. These are the people who push you to be your best. They pick you up after you try and fail. They are always there for you.

Motivation comes from you. Others can encourage you to exercise, for example, but if you don't have the motivation to exercise there's nothing they can do to get you on a bike. You have to look to yourself for that. I didn't get the encouragement I needed when I was in school. Because I have dyslexia, most people believed it would prevent me from achieving my goal that, at the time, was to attend college.

As I said earlier, I was in special needs classes, back then they were labeled as "learning disability" classes and my teachers, based on their experience, didn't believe I was going to be able to attend college. They discouraged me from applying to the college of my dreams and instead encouraged me to attend a school that offered special programs for those with similar disabilities.

Encouragement became Motivation

I had to begin relying less on others' encouragement. That didn't mean I stopped looking to others for support, but, over time, I had to look more to myself. I focused on my goal and what I needed to do to reach it; doing my absolute best in high school; doing the extra work necessary; staying motivated. I wouldn't have graduated from high school and my chosen college without both encouragement and motivation.

Finding encouragement. Building motivation.

I still look to a few trusted people in my life for encouragement, especially my mentor. I have found ways to stay motivated. It can be very difficult at times, but that's normal for everyone.

I read stories about how others succeeded, especially those who overcame difficulties. I wanted to know everything about how they achieved their success. I read magazines and listened to motivational CDs, which was particularly helpful for me, because then I didn't have to read.

Who and what will keep you motivated?

Seek individuals and organizations that will encourage you as your motivation grows. It may be your parents, a teacher or guidance counselor, your pastor, or a friend. You may also find other sources of encouragement, like a favorite song that speaks to you; a peer group of like-minded people, or inspirational quotes. Listen to the stories of how those who inspire you succeeded.

If you have only a bit of motivation, make it count. Find that initial source of encouragement and build from there. Eventually, you will find your motivation and look more to yourself. It's time for you to step up and stay motivated.

EmpowerME Journal Topic

Describe what most motivates you.

_____

_____

_____

_____

_____

_____

_____

_____

"A mission statement is
not something you write
overnight…

but fundamentally, your
mission statement becomes
your constitution,

the solid expression of your
vision and values. It becomes
the criterion by which you
measure everything else
in your life."

Stephen Covey
American Educator

—

7

Personal Mission Statement

What's your life mission?

It's not an easy question to answer, but an important one. You can talk about your aspirations and goals all day, but when you write them down, they become, well, more real. It's a starting point to living the life you want.

When you write a personal mission statement, you're clarifying what you want to accomplish and how, and committing to it. Businesses and nonprofit organizations develop mission statements for the same reason.

What is a personal mission statement?

Most students, and adults, don't realize the importance of writing their personal mission statements. It's more than just your goals. Your mission statement will help you sort out your priorities and how you want to live your life. It may include short-term and long-term goals, or lifelong aspirations. It becomes a guide and provides direction, which comes from you, not someone else.

There's no right or wrong way to approach your personal mission statement, or what it should include. Everyone's mission statement is going to be different. What's important is to write it down.

Topics your personal mission statement may include:

- Career
- Community service
- Education
- Faith and spirituality
- Family and personal relationships
- How you want to live your life
- Personal attributes, such as honesty, loyalty and dedication
- Sports

Writing your mission statement

I wrote my first personal mission statement when I was in seventh grade at the guidance of my teacher and mentor. I sort of knew what my goals were, but never wrote them down. I made a commitment to myself by writing my mission statement.

It took only a couple hours to write mine. I didn't follow a process.

I talked a lot about my goals with my mentor, so it was in my head. It was up to me to write it down, which was the most difficult part for me because dyslexia makes writing very challenging—scary. If you want to use a more structured approach, I've offered tips here and there are websites that have more suggestions on developing personal mission statement.

The focus of my mission statement probably didn't seem realistic to anyone except me. I read slower and it was difficult—often impossible—for me to verbalize the right answers. I was called stupid by my peers. I was a frustrated bully. My mission statement helped me focus all my efforts on achieving my goals, especially attending Marquette University—and proving wrong everyone who didn't believe I could.

It's only the first step

Your personal mission statement is only the first step. You won't achieve your goals just by writing them down and through wishful thinking. Now you need to create an action plan by identifying and taking all the little steps needed to fulfill your mission statement.

Review it regularly

You may get so wrapped up in our day-to-day activities, you forget why you're doing what you're doing. Your mission statement helps you focus on what you're striving toward. Everything you do today either leads you toward or away from your goals.

Review your mission statement as often as you need to. I reviewed mine every year or so. It may be helpful to review yours more regularly: monthly, weekly, or even daily. Over time, your aspirations may change. Don't hesitate to update your mission statement to reflect your new hopes and dreams. At the very least, I'd suggest updating your mission statement annually.

It really can change your life

I didn't realize how of my personal mission statement changed my life until I was out of college. Now, I look at it and realize it really helped me focus on my life goals. I learned strategies to help overcome dyslexia and graduate from Marquette University with my bachelor's degree in Business. I now have a new personal mission statement that helps me focus on my current goals and aspirations.

EmpowerME Journal Topic

Write your mission statement here.

"It is our choices…
that show what we
truly are, far more
than our abilities."

J. K. Rowling
British Novelist
—

Academic Success or Failure:
It's Up to You

Your success or failure in school at any level comes with a simple event in your life – a decision. In high school, making the wrong decision about three key activities can devastate your future. These three activities are:

1. Attending class
2. Taking notes in class
3. Studying after class

If you noticed a pattern in the three key activities, they all revolve around class – the decision you make before class, the decision you make during class, and the decision you make after class.

Attending Class

At the start of every day, deciding to eat a good breakfast can make possibly challenging day, exciting. In the same way, simply attending class can make an exciting day, rewarding. The importance of being present in class cannot be stressed enough.

Attending class makes you present. Yet, being present means being active and engaged by following along, asking questions, and answering questions when called upon by the instructor or teacher.

Taking Notes in Class

The truth of the matter is it takes attention and effort to take notes in class. In fact, it takes attention and effort to do pretty much anything in life. And yet, many students appear in class and sit there, not taking notes until the review for the exam or test. Here, the instructor or teacher gives an overview of what was covered during the class periods, and expects you to utilize your notes to study. Notes you haven't taken for weeks. Your grades suffer. Therefore, you suffer.

There is an art and science to taking notes. Since you cannot record everything said in class, I suggest you follow the Cornell Notes Method of taking notes. Go to Wikipedia or your favorite search site and search "Cornell Notes" for directions on how to create a document template.

Studying After Class

Okay, I admit it – I had trouble studying after class. There. I said it. Also, I had trouble taking notes in class due to my dyslexia. I had trouble going to class because I knew I had trouble reading and writing, and if the teacher called on me, I look and sound like a fool. So, I took my own worst advice and went to class when I felt like going to class.

I was wrong.

One of the most difficult parts of being to college was to create the habit of going to class, taking notes and studying. Notice a pattern here? Habits I did not set for myself in high school later came back in the form of difficulty in college. It was difficult for me getting to college, and it was difficult for me getting though class, because I had not let my thoughts turn to action, and become habits.

It is important to consciously make an effort to show up. How well you understand the information in class is based on how well you take notes. Studying after class can have an effect on your entire academic career.

The first step is always the hardest, yet if you follow through with all of the steps, you will achieve academic success.

I can't stress enough the importance of having individuals who support you and encourage you. I've described my reading and writing challenges earlier in this book, and without a doubt, I've connected with people who have encouraged me to share my knowledge with students, empowering them to be successful. One of those people I've leaned on for this book is Dr. Ken Harris. His profession as a leader, college administrator and educator has allowed him to work with a large number of college students. He's shared with me the many students he's known who have been close to their goal of attending college, and almost gave in to obstacles and challenges in their path.

Dr. Harris told me the story of a friend of his who hadn't been in college for 15 years and wanted to finish his bachelor's degree. Dr. Harris helped his friend find a school, pick a major and register for his first series of classes.

On the first day of class about an hour before the class started, his friend had convinced himself that going back to school after so much time was a bad idea. So, the friend called Dr. Harris and said, "I've decided I'm not going to go to school. I'm probably not smart enough and it's gonna be hard."

Dr. Harris, in what I think was a smart move, said, "Go to class one night and stay the entire class period. Then go home and go to bed. If you wake up tomorrow and still want to quit, go ahead and quit." The friend replied, "No, I'm not going." Dr. Harris said, "Tell you what, I'll come to class with you and sit the first hour." The friend agreed, met him at the school, and went to the first class. The decision turned out to be the best decision this friend ever made.

Two years after beginning, the friend graduated from the university summa cum laude with a 4.0 perfect grade point average. Dr. Harris told me his friend based his academic success on his decision to go to class, making sure he paid attention by taking good notes, and then setting up a regimen of studying on a regular basis. I share and continue to repeat these three activities because they can lead to academic success. Academic success is important in whatever area you decide to study in high school and college, or learning a trade. It goes to show, in the end, academic success is based on the decisions you make and the activities you complete. Academic success or failure? You choose.

It's up to you.

EmpowerME Journal Topic

Describe how you plan to turn failure into success.

"

"It's all about people.

It's about networking and
being nice to people
and not burning any bridges.

Your [work] is going to
impress, but in the end
it is people that are
going to hire you."

Mike Davidson
Author and Businessman

—

9

Networking

I would not have succeeded in school or my professional life without networking. It isn't something only business people do when looking for a job. Everyone should network, all the time, even you. The sooner you start, the better.

My grandmother pounded into my head, "It's not what you know. It's who you know." I believe that's mostly true. You may have the best grades and leadership skills, or excel at sports, but if nobody knows it, what good will it do you? Your accomplishments are only part of the equation. Who you know and how you present yourself are just as important.

For now, networking is about introducing yourself, and making connections with people from whom you can learn or possibly gain assistance. Networking can help you get into the college of your choice, learn about various careers, and build valuable personal and professional skills you'll use throughout your life.

It can be awkward for everyone

You're probably going to feel awkward as you start building your networking skills. I did. That's a natural feeling.

I met a professional I respected while in college, who later became my mentor. I asked him to introduce me to everyone he knew. He took me to meetings and events, and although it's what I wanted, these were new, uncomfortable settings for me. He kept encouraging me, "Keep coming and, eventually, they'll get to know you. And always bring your business cards, you never know who you're going to meet."

Networking will push you outside of your comfort zone. I was uncomfortable at first, but over time, it got easier. There are still times I'm uncomfortable, but I've learned to force myself. I'm always learning better ways to network.

Where to network

There are basically two types of networking: groups and one-on-one. A good place to start is in settings with people you're already acquainted: sports groups; fundraising events; church, synagogue or mosque functions; or any other place you would already be. Your goal is to practice walking up to someone you don't know, introduce yourself, and start a conversation.

If you know someone that attends professional networking groups, you may want to ask them if you can tag along. Ask them to introduce you to a few people, then strike out on your own and start introducing yourself.

One-on-one networking

One-on-one meetings are generally with someone specifically you want to meet. It could be someone who graduated from the college you want to attend, is in a career you'd like to consider, or you respect and simply want to meet.

First, find out if you already know someone who can introduce you. Ask around. Maybe your friend's brother, for example, didn't graduate from the college you want to attend, but he may know someone who did. You never know until you ask.

Don't be afraid to pick up the phone and call the person you want to meet with or send them an email. Tell them why you're contacting them. Most people will be willing to give you an hour of their time. Before you meet with them, write down the questions you'd like to ask, and have paper and pen ready to take notes. I suggest you meet at their office.

Start now

Find your motivation and get out there. Introduce yourself. Meet lots of people in different settings. It gets easier with practice. You'll meet some incredible people, who may be able to give you a bit of advice or a helping hand. You'll be amazed to find out you have more in common with others than you may have thought.

Finally, let me leave you with what I call the Seven Benefits of Networking:

1. Build your self-confidence
2. Find internships
3. Gain experience introducing yourself and others
4. Interact with others in professional settings
5. Learn about people from different backgrounds
6. Learn about various industries and types of work
7. Practice keeping a conversation going

EmpowerME Journal Topic

Describe the one person with whom you would like to network and why.

"

"A real conversation always contains an invitation.

You are inviting another person to reveal herself or himself to you, to tell you who they are and what they want."

David Whyte
English Poet
—

Keeping the Conversation Going

I regularly hear excuses for why someone didn't follow up, and whether its students or professionals, it always disappoints me. It's so easy, but so often forgotten.

According to Merriam-Webster, follow up is "a continuation of something that has already been started." Someone hands you an apple. You thank them. That's follow up. It's that easy.

If you say you're going to follow up with someone, and you don't, you're not demonstrating your reliability or your interest. This applies to any situation in your life, from personal relationships and school, to clubs and jobs. If the ball is in your court don't drop it! I suggest following up as quickly as you can, ideally within two days – while the meeting, conversation, or commitment is still fresh.

When to follow up

There are many situations in which following up is necessary. Always follow up after:

An interview. You'll stand out among other candidates. Send a thank you email or make a phone call to offer your gratitude for their time.

Meeting someone new. You want them to remember you and what you talked about, don't you? This is important as you build your network of people who may be willing and able to help you out. Let them know you're interested in staying in contact, and that you will touch base periodically. This leaves the door open for future contact.

Someone did something for you. It common courtesy to thank someone, such as when someone made an introduction for you.

Someone gave you something. Thank people for what they gave you, whether it's information, a letter of recommendation, a suggestion or idea, or their time.

A conversation or meeting. Avoid misunderstandings and make sure you're both on the same page by summarizing what you talked about. It's also a way to remind them what they agreed to do, and what you agreed to do.

You took action. If someone opened a door for you with an introduction, keep them in the loop. People appreciate knowing you made the connection, how you're moving forward, and whether the introduction was a good one or not. If you keep them posted, they're more likely to make more introductions, because you treated the first one seriously and professionally.

How to follow up

There are several ways to follow up. The most common are sending a letter, note card, or email, or calling. The best choice depends on the situation and the person:

Send a letter. This is the most formal method of following up. It's appropriate after more formal activities, like an interview or if the person is of importance, such as an elected official or a corporate executive. Be sure to spell and grammar check (because I've been there) prior to sending your letter in the mail.

Send a note card. These are a bit less formal and are appropriate when you want to thank someone. They can also be sent after an interview, when meeting someone new, or thanking someone for an informal meeting. Sending thank you notes is a lost art, so stand out by sending one.

Send an email. Emails are informal and can be used when summarizing a meeting or when communicating with someone with whom you have already built a relationship. It may also be appropriate when you just met someone informally, like at a basketball game.

Make a phone call. Use this method when you have several questions you'd like to ask or have information to give. Calling is good when you're confirming an appointment. Calling is the best way to stand out, especially as a young adult.

I stress the importance of following up with the students with whom I work. It's an important lesson. Start now, and following up will become a valuable habit the rest of your life.

Ask yourself…is there anyone to follow up with today?

EmpowerME Journal Topic

Describe the one person you are most fearful to speak with, and tell how you will overcome this fear.

"Mentoring is a brain to pick,
and ear to listen,
and a push in the right direction."

John C. Crosby
Politician

—

11

Mentoring Basics
I Have A Mentor – Now What?

Short and sweet, having prepared questions will make meeting anyone easier. Before looking at the next chapter, write several down at least four additional questions and put them in your pocket so you don't forget. The next chapter will give you additional questions you can ask when you're networking or when you meet with your mentor. If any of the questions in the next chapter are the same as the ones you come up with, force yourself to come up with new questions so you have a total of 20 questions. This is only a start.

One other quick note for you to think about regarding mentors. Be sure you understand how and when you and your mentor will communicate. It is important to respect your mentor's time both personally and professionally. Understanding that emergencies happen, be sure you are both clear about communication.

EmpowerME Journal Topic

Describe what you believe to be the most important thing to do after meeting someone.

"The art and science of
asking questions
is the source of all
knowledge."

Thomas Berger
American Novelist
—

12

Questions for Your Mentor
Play 20 Questions

Here are 16 of the first 20 questions you should ask your mentor. Of course, you need to create an additional four questions to ask, for a total of 20 questions.

1. What was your experience getting into college?

2. Did you consider attending any other college?

3. What was the most valuable thing you learned in college?

4. What was your first job out of college?

5. How can I best prepare for my first job out of college?

6. How did you get to this point in your career?

7. What was your worst failure in school? Career?

8. What advice would you give me if I were considering going into (the industry or job you'd like to know more about)?

9. What's a typical workday like for you?

10. What are the most important skills needed to do your job?

11. What experiences or classes do you think would be most valuable?

12. Do you have any suggestions for how I can get more experience?

13. In your industry, where's the greatest demand for employees?

14. Is there anything you wish someone had taught you earlier in your career?

15. What's the most valuable advice your mentor gave you?

16. Is there anyone else you think I should talk to?

17. _____

18. _____

19. _____

20. _____

EmpowerME Journal Topic

Describe the one most challenging question you have, and how you will pursue an answer.

_____

_____

_____

_____

_____

_____

_____

_____

"

"Planning is bringing the future into the present so that you can do something about it now."

Alan Lakein
Author

—

13

Planning on Success

Taking time to review your goals is always something you should find time to do. If you have a personal mission statement, get it out and see how you're doing on working toward your goals. If you don't have one, it's time to put your goals on paper. If you don't plan on where you want to go, you'll end up somewhere, you just can't be sure where. ***Visit JoeVillmow.com to view my personal mission statement created in the 7th grade.***

Now that you have your goals in front of you, no matter how much or how little you accomplished last year, you can plan for greater success in the coming year. Benjamin Franklin said it well, "By failing to prepare, you are preparing to fail." So, plan to succeed.

The Pizza Plan: Creating your personal action plan

Your personal action plan is like eating a pizza. Your goals are the ingredients that make up an extra large, family-sized pizza. You're hungry to achieve your goals. You'd like to devour the entire pizza in one sitting and accomplish your goals all at one time. But, you can't eat an entire pizza in one bite.

Let's say your goal, your pizza, is to be accepted into college.

Cut the pizza into manageable-sized pieces

Identify small, manageable tasks that will move you toward your goal. Make sure they're specific and realistic. You can eat the entire pizza by cutting it into smaller, bite-size pieces, and eating one at a time. If the slices are too big, achieving your goal will still be overwhelming.

You may want to complete a dozen college applications, but you're not going to get them all done in one sitting. That's unrealistic — the slice is way too big. If you try to eat too much at one time, or too fast, you'll choke and you may give up. The same is true for your goals.

What are the different slices into which you could cut your pizza? Do you know what colleges to which you'd like to apply? One slice could be researching colleges. Another could be the classes you're taking now. Are they challenging you? Are you gaining the knowledge you need for the major you're interested in? Another slice could be gaining the skills that will help you stand out among other applicants. Are you volunteering in your community? How are you gaining leadership skills?

You know you're going to be asked to submit an essay with your application. Start writing it. That's a slice. But, you can chop that into smaller bites, too: research what makes an essay stand out; find examples; jot down some notes on what you'd like your essay to include; and begin to outline your essay.

When to eat each slice

Do some slices need to be eaten before others? Research comes before submitting applications. Taking the right class leads to the knowledge you need to acquire before deciding to which colleges you'd like to apply.

Remember, you can't eat the entire pizza in one sitting. Create a timeline for eating each piece, taking each bite, and achieving each smaller task. If there's no deadline, or due date, it likely won't ever get done. That's why I continue to set deadlines for myself.

Start with your deadline and work backwards. Your first application is due in nine months, so work back from there. What do you need to do the week before? The month before? What can you do today to help you achieve your goal? Create a checklist so you can see what lies ahead and what you've already accomplished. It's satisfying to cross something off your list.

Everyday ask yourself, what can I do today to help me reach my goal?

Keep eating

Over time, you may need to cut your pizza differently. Or, you may find one slice was a bit too hard to stomach, so you cut the remaining slices into even smaller pieces. Things change or get us off track for a while, so your timeline may need to be modified. Don't be discouraged. One thing won't change: your goal.

Every success starts with a clear idea of what you want. Your pizza. Plan your success by cutting the pizza into slices and bites you can eat over time. Eat a piece, then another piece, then another. Over time, you'll devour the entire pizza. The most important thing is to stay hungry!

EmpowerME Journal Topic

Describe the first thing you will do when you receive your first full-time job.

"What is the recipe for successful achievement? In my mind there are just four essential ingredients:

Choose a career you love, give it the best there is in you, seize your opportunities, and be a member of the team."

Benjamin Franklin Fairless
American Steel Company Executive

—

14

Andres

A few years ago, while on the Marquette University College of Business board, we held one of the many networking events, and a student, Andres was one of the students chosen to network with a number of Marquette University alumni. Alumni get together to discuss accounting, economics, finance, and other business topics.

At events, I tend to watch the room. I'm a people person, so I read a person's body language. Andres' body language said he was intimidated. He stood in the corner. I believe this is normal, since students can be intimidated around professionals who act and dress the part.

I approached Andres and introduced myself to him. I could tell he was a shy person. He knew he was in a great atmosphere, yet I believed he didn't have the two skills needed to be comfortable at this event. He needed encouragement and confidence; two skills needed to build relationships. This would, in turn, help Andres build a conversation with those in attendance.

Having to use self-encouragement and my own personal confidence, I came up to him and I said, "Hello. What's your name?" We talked back and forth. I told him a little bit about myself and the foundation's mission. I shared my story, similar to what I wrote in this book, and told him I was looking for students to assist me with the foundation.

Andres said he was very impressed with my story saying, "I want to follow up with you because I think you could help one of my brothers." I'm thinking to myself, "I'm trying to help him out, but in his mind, he's already taking care of his family and one of his younger brothers." I found this admirable, so I gave him my business card expecting him to follow up with me.

Andres was great because he knew how to follow up, and within two hours he followed up, thanked me for the time spent connecting, and did not ask for advice or personal help, yet continued to discuss how to help his brother. While helping his brother was a noble cause, Andres did not understand that to help others, a person has to help themselves first. He became my first student and I became his mentor. For me this was a moment to pass the torch of knowledge as my mentor, Lupe Martinez did many years ago.

Together, we attended networking events. He accepted my challenge to volunteer. I would like to say he did it of his own free will, but I had to do some nudging to get him going in the right direction, much the same way others did for me. Eventually, Andres learned the "what" and the "why" of networking.

Many of the tasks I assigned Andres to do for the foundation were so he could learn from his experiences. Some of the assignments included failing. Doing many of these projects allowed him the opportunity to grow and learn.

Reading this book is the equivalent of completing similar assignment in an effort to show you how to grow and learn.

EmpowerME Journal Topic

Describe your first successful accomplishment and its impact on your life.

_____

_____

_____

_____

_____

_____

_____

_____

"

"The key is to keep company
only with people who
uplift you,
whose presence calls
forth your best."

Epictetus
Philosopher

—

The Compound Effect

Similar to Andres, everyone that comes into my foundation, I consider family. I want the best for them. One of my mentors, Darren Hardy, former CEO and Publisher of *Success Magazine*, has a book called, *The Compound Effect*. In his book, he talked about to make money, and how we will make money later in life. Also, he discusses people like me – entrepreneurs.

Think of it this way: Darren interviews other successful people. He tells his story and their story. He takes the knowledge of others and transfers it to the reader. The reader, namely me and you, take it and give it to others, and in my case I gave the knowledge to Andres.

There are two words that describe this process: mentoring and networking. I take a students, expose them to the skills of networking through mentoring, thereby building my own compound effect.

Remember how I shared earlier in the book that your experiences become your story? Well, although he may have been a bit introverted at the first Marquette networking function, now Andres has a story to tell. His story is motivating and uplifting. His story motivates students into joining the foundation and learning these skills. Andres now shares his story and my story, helping student develop and grow their own story – the compound effect of mentoring. It doesn't matter what race, color, or ethnicity you are, this can be replicated with anyone. The important item to remember is it comes down to you making the decision to receiving the motivation, and giving motivation to others.

I met my mentors through networking, which led to me being mentored. I started with Marquette University students. When you are going to network and mentor, start from a familiar and comfortable place. For me, it was Marquette University.

Consider what can occur when a person mentors students in their teenage years and young adult years. Andres, who is still fairly young, mentors students in my foundation. So I mean, he's still young, and if you take into account all the other students in my foundation, the impact is could be incredible.

If I start with 10 students, who go out the next year and each of them mentors a group of 10 students, this amounts to 100 students impacted through mentoring. This same 100 students take on 10 students each, and those students take on 10 students each, over just five years the impact would be one million students. Now, I realize this is a huge goal, yet think of what 100,000 positively impacted students would mean for a community the size of Cleveland or Indianapolis or Milwaukee? This is my pizza, our pizza. Every success you experience, helps us all to stay hungry.

I wrote this book to give you the template for the skills needed to network and be mentored. Follow the template. The decision is up to you. Help me to help and motivate you to make more successful leaders.

The template is to be used over a lifetime. I admit to the fact that I thought I knew it all once I graduated from Marquette University. Yet, here I am *still* being mentored. I had to make the realization that learning really is a lifelong journey. Every day, every hour, every minute and every second you are learning from others. Even when you learn what not to do, you are learning.

Additionally, you may believe you need a mentor in your field, and believe this to be completely wrong. You're always learning from other people. Having information about other fields and careers is important because you may need to or want to change careers. You want to have mentors from all walks of professional life.

You need to know a mentors' story, get advice on their struggle, and learn how to become successful. Also, you need to understand there are failures in life. Therefore, you learn how to avoid the potholes in life. Avoiding potholes is perhaps one of the most important aspects of learning, while understanding that every now and then you will hit a pothole and cause damage. Your recover from failure builds persistence and resilience in your life.

As a sophomore, Andres met the CEO of a Fortune 500 company. I showed Andres how to apply the principles given in this book through coaching and mentoring. He parlayed this meeting and what he learned into an internship at a top accounting firm. It should be understood that not many people get internships at this type of firm.

Eventually, Andres came to know and be well-acquainted with the managing partner at this firm, which opened up additional doors. The lesson here is if you want to have a career similar to someone, you have to be around them, meet them, and continue to surround yourself with great, successful authentic people.

Authentic people will push you, and if you want to be successful, they can make it happen. I am authentic, and I am here to push you in the same way I pushed Andres to succeed.

"Stay positive and happy. Work hard and don't give up hope.

Be open to criticism and keep learning.

Surround yourself with happy, warm and genuine people."

Tena Desae
Indian Actress

—

16

Conclusion

As this book draws a close, I want you to know this book is about my story. It's about who I was, who I became, and who I am today. This book is about giving you the skills needed today that may not being taught in school, or even in your home. This book is written to give you a starting point.

Reading this book will not take you to the pinnacle of success because it's up to you to get there for yourself. Reading this book affords you the opportunity to succeed by listening to my failures, my success and my struggles. Through high school, along the way, you're going to have failures. When you go to college, or get a job, you'll have to overcome obstacles both personal and professional. The skills learned in this book and everything I'm sharing is for you to prepare yourself for what lies ahead – life.

Imagine right at this moment, you've finished this book. The first thing I suggest you do is to work to develop your personal mission statement. Your mission statement is the beginning of pursuing your dreams. Your mission statement reminds you of what you want in life. As your wants change, it's important that your personal mission statement changes month after month; year after year. Change and growth occurs because you communicate, grow, and network with other people. In high school, odds are in your favor to change and grow. Of course, college is no different. Change is inevitable.

As you change and grow, maturity will take over. You learn. You listen. You ask questions. The personal mission statement accompanies you as you accomplish and grow. You grow, the personal mission statement grows with you. It becomes a life plan; a map of sorts.

As in business, you have to have a business plan. The business plan also accompanies your business as you accomplish tasks and grow your business. How are you going to start making money and growing your business? How are you going to be successful in life? What steps must be taken to reach your dreams? Your personal mission statement, your experiences, and this book can act as your road map to track your growth and furnishes a plan on how to move forward.

EmpowerME Journal Topic

Describe the most positive event that has occurred in your life.

_____

_____

_____

_____

_____

_____

_____

_____

About The Author

As a child growing up in Brown Deer, Wisconsin, Joe Villmow faced academic and personal challenges, including dyslexia and traumatic experiences. In grade school, Joe met a mentor who encouraged him to develop a personal mission statement, one that would later change his life. He achieved that mission – to graduate from Marquette University – where he earned a Bachelor of Science in Business Administration in 2006. Joe is the owner of four successful and growing companies. From the successes of his businesses, Joe decided to start the EmpowerMe Foundation, whose mission helps high school and undergraduate students develop valuable skills critical to their academic, professional and life successes. EmpowerMe accomplishes this through programs focused on: identifying one's values and life mission, professional mentoring and networking, community service, and financial support. Following the footsteps of his mentors, Joe teaches students the same critical business and life skills that led to his own personal success. At the core of who he is, Joe's admiration and love for his community drives his desire to serve. Joe actively supports the community by serving on the boards of directors of UMOS (United Migrant Opportunity Services), Marquette University Business Alumni Board, and Marquette University Ethnic Alumni Association, FBI Citizens.

Joe currently mentors high-school students at Oconomowoc High School, Waukesha West High School, Carmen High School and college students at Marquette University.